OREGON
portrait of a state

OREGON
portrait of a state

RICK SCHAFER

GRAPHIC ARTS BOOKS

Photographs © MMII by Rick Schafer

Library of Congress Control Number: 2005929668
International Standard Book Number: 978-1-55868-909-1

Graphic Arts Books, an imprint of
Graphic Arts Center Publishing Company
P.O. Box 10306, Portland, Oregon 97296-0306
503/226-2402; www.gacpc.com

The five-dot logo is a registered trademark of
Graphic Arts Center Publishing Company.

President: Charles M. Hopkins
Associate Publisher: Douglas A. Pfeiffer
Editorial Staff: Timothy W. Frew, Tricia Brown, Kathy Howard, Jean Bond-Slaughter
Production Staff: Richard L. Owsiany, Heather Doornink
Cover Design: Elizabeth Watson
Interior Design: Jean Andrews

Printed in The United States of America

FRONT COVER: ❘ A storm leaves Crater Lake a brilliant turquoise.
BACK COVER: ❘ The Painted Hills, in John Day Fossil Beds National Monument, are
splashed with areas of pink, red, bronze, tan, and black—with yellow and green added in spring.
◀◀ Mount Hood, seen from Jonsrud Point, hovers over the fog-filled Willamette Valley.
◀ The sheltered cove at Fogarty Creek State Recreation Area draws sightseers
for picnicking, bird-watching, and tide pooling.

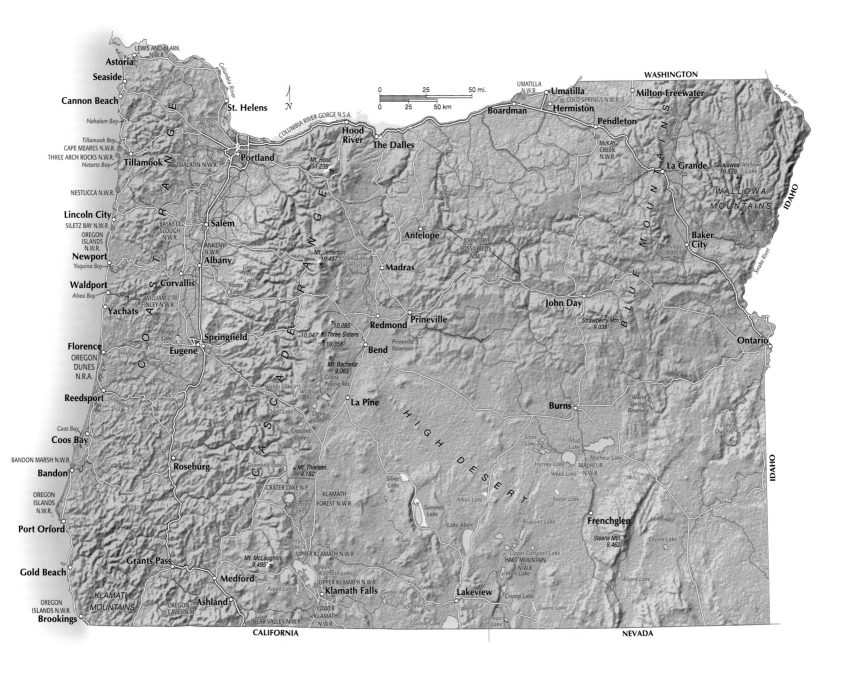

LEWIS AND CLARK N.W.R.

Astoria

Seaside

Cannon Beach

WASHINGTON

St. Helens

UMATILLA N.W.R.

Umatilla

COLD SPRINGS N.W.R.

Milton-Freewater

Boardman

Hermiston

Pendleton

Nehalem Bay

Tillamook Bay

CAPE MEARES N.W.R.

THREE ARCH ROCKS N.W.R.

Netarts Bay

Tillamook

TUALATIN N.W.R.

Portland

Hood River

The Dalles

McKAY CREEK N.W.R.

La Grande

Sacajawea 9,839'

Wallowa Lake

Mt. Hood 11,239'

WALLOWA MOUNTAINS

NESTUCCA N.W.R.

Salem

Lincoln City

SILETZ BAY N.W.R.

OREGON ISLANDS N.W.R.

BASKETT SLOUGH N.W.R.

ANKENY N.W.R.

Antelope

JOHN DAY FOSSIL BEDS N.M.

Baker City

Phillips Lake

Newport

Yaquina Bay

Albany

Mt. Jefferson 10,497'

Lake Simtustus

Madras

Waldport

Alsea Bay

WILLIAM L. FINLEY N.W.R.

Corvallis

Green Peter Lake

Foster Lake

Lake Billy Chinook

Yachats

Fern Ridge Lake

Springfield

10,085'

10,047' Three Sisters

10,358'

Redmond

Prineville

John Day

Strawberry Mtn. 9,038'

Florence

OREGON DUNES N.R.A.

Eugene

Siuslaw R.

Mt. Bachelor 9,065'

Crane Prairie Res.

Bend

Prineville Reservoir

Ontario

Waldo Lake

Wickiup Res.

Umpqua R.

Reedsport

Odell Lake

Davis Lake

La Pine

Burns

Warm Springs Reservoir

Coos Bay

Crescent Lake

Lake Owyhee

Coos Bay

BANDON MARSH N.W.R.

Roseburg

Diamond Lake

Mt. Thielsen 9,182'

Silver Lake

Mud Lake

Malheur Lake

Bandon

Silver Lake

Harney Lake

MALHEUR N.W.R.

Weed Lake

Foster Lake

OREGON ISLANDS N.W.R.

CRATER LAKE N.P.

KLAMATH FOREST N.W.R.

Crater Lake

Alkali Lake

Lake Abert

Port Orford

Bluejoint Lake

Frenchglen

Steens Mtn. 9,462'

Coyote Lake

KLAMATH MOUNTAINS

Grants Pass

Mt. McLaughlin 9,495'

Summer Lake

UPPER KLAMATH N.W.R.

Upper Campbell Lake

HART MOUNTAIN N.W.R.

Gold Beach

OREGON CAVES N.M.

Ashland

Medford

Upper Klamath Lake

UPPER KLAMATH N.W.R.

Agency Lake

Aspen Lake

HART MOUNTAIN N.W.R.

Alvord Lake

OREGON ISLANDS N.W.R.

Klamath Falls

LOWER KLAMATH N.W.R.

BEAR VALLEY N.W.R.

Gerber Res.

Drews Res.

Goose Lake

Lakeview

Crump Lake

Coleman Lake

Guano Lake

Brookings

CALIFORNIA

NEVADA

Columbia River

COLUMBIA RIVER GORGE N.S.A.

Sturgeon Lake

Willamette R.

CASCADE RANGE

COAST RANGE

BLUE MOUNTAINS

HIGH DESERT

Snake River

Grande Ronde R.

Snake River

WASHINGTON

IDAHO

IDAHO

0   25   50 mi.
0   25   50 km

◄ Evergreen trees line lava beds along the McKenzie-Santiam Scenic Byway.
▲ Wheel ruts lead to an abandoned farmhouse in a Wasco County wheat field.
Early settlers, frequently undercapitalized, sometimes abandoned their homesteads
because they were unable to survive a drought, or because they could not stand the isolation.
►► One of the West's best rainbow trout fishing rivers, the Metolius flows from
an underground spring at the base of Black Butte.

▲ Hug Point is a small wayside off Highway 101, south of Cannon Beach.
Until the highway was built in 1936, the beach all along the coast served as a
road, first for stagecoaches, and later, automobiles. Hug Point's rock ledge was hewed
out to become part of that "road." Now, it's a great place for walking, sea-watching,
and exploring the two caves around the point—but only during low tide!

▲ CLOCKWISE FROM TOP LEFT: ◖ The Willamette River and Hawthorne Bridge set off Portland's skyline.
◖ Sheppards Dell Falls is one of many beautiful vistas along the Historic Columbia River Highway.
◖ Wave-watching is a favorite pastime at Rocky Creek State Wayside, on Oregon's central coast.
◖ Nestled beneath low hills, barns overlook a Wasco County alfalfa field.
▶▶ Mount Jefferson soars 10,495 feet above sea level.

11

▲ The "Golden Pioneer" has topped the rotunda of Oregon's
capitol in Salem since completion of the building in 1938. Created by
Ulric Ellerhusen, the gold-plated, hollow statue is twenty-three feet high and weighs
eight and one-half tons. A 121-step spiral staircase leads to the base of the statue.
▶ Colorful hot air balloons often dot the sky above the patchwork of
fields and streams between Newberg and St. Paul.

◄ The depths of Wallowa Lake portray
a softer version of the solid Wallowa Mountains.
▲ On Mount Howard, Royal Purple Viewpoint offers panoramas
of the Wallowa Mountains and Eagle Cap Wilderness. The Wallowas
are unique in the state: they are granitic in composition rather
than of volcanic origin or the result of lava flows.

▲ Looking across the Columbia River to Washington from
near the Oregon town of Arlington, the river may seem quiet and
peaceful, but that tranquil appearance hides a potentially dangerous enemy.
▶ The Ladd Marsh Wildlife Refuge is located in the southwest corner of
the Grande Ronde Valley. The refuge hosts wetlands critical to
nesting and migrating birds, including the sandhill crane,
American avocet, and ring-necked duck, among others.

▲ A bull rider loses his grip at the Pendleton Round-Up.
In 1909, the Fourth of July celebration in Pendleton included bronc
riding and horse racing, and the idea was conceived that a round-up should be
held each year. Numerous events are scheduled, from the World's Most Unique Indian
Pageant to Steer Wrestling, Wild Cow Milking, and Barrel Racing. Each year, the
round-up attracts some fifty thousand visitors from around the world.

▲ Native American children also participate at the Pendleton Round-Up.
From the beginning, Indians have been an important factor in the success of the
round-up, thanks originally to excellent relations between Major Lee Moorehouse,
superintendent of the Umatilla Reservation Agency; Roy Bishop, Round-Up Indian
Director; and Poker Jim, an Indian chief and nephew of Chief Joseph.

▲ The Narrows, a channel connecting Harney and Malheur
Lakes in the Malheur National Wildlife Refuge, has flooded so extensively
some years that both lakes have run together to become a single body of water.
▶ The steep, rocky landscape of a canyon of Steens Mountain offers a desolate look.
Formed by faulting rather than volcanic action, the mountain rises 9,670 feet.
▶▶ Central Oregon's wheat adds beauty to nature's rolling hills.

◄ The setting sun is reflected off clouds,
painting a brilliant picture over the Pacific Ocean.

▲ The St. John's Bridge traverses the Willamette River north of
downtown Portland. Constructed in 1931, its main span is 1,207 feet long.

►► Heceta Head Lighthouse, completed in 1894 at a cost of
$180,000, towers 205 feet above the ocean.

◄ Off Cannon Beach and just south of Haystack Rock, two
tall, narrow rocks known as the Needles poke holes in the sky.
▲▲ Cannon Beach's Haystack Rock rises 235 feet out of the sea at low tide.
▲ Cape Kiwanda's sandstone cliffs, soaring about a hundred feet above
the ocean, set off the "other" Haystack Rock, about a mile
offshore and reaching 327 feet above the ocean floor.

▲ The town of Cannon Beach offers almost as much interest
to visitors as do the ever-changing moods of the ocean itself. Here,
colorful hanging baskets vie for attention with "open" and "espresso" signs.
Constructed about 1935, this building first served as a pharmacy. The tradition of flower
baskets, begun in the 1960s by the shopkeepers' wives, is continued by the city today.
▶ At sunset, seagulls gather in a small stream on Ecola State Park's Indian Beach.

◄ Newport Harbor's early morning tranquillity belies the busyness
that will be evident later in the day when whale-watching and sight-seeing cruises,
along with commercial and charter fishing boats, all conspire to bring the waterfront alive.
▲ An exposed root system creates an interesting pattern at Shore Acres State Park. Once the grand
estate of pioneer timber baron Louis Simpson, Shore Acres incorporates a surprising
blend of natural and constructed features, including formal gardens
that showcase plants and flowers from around the world.

▲ The Jessie M. Honeyman Memorial State Park,
south of Florence, is noted for its high sand dunes and
beautiful rhododendron blooms. Day uses for the two freshwater
lakes in the park include swimming, fishing, and boating.

▲ In addition to seals, for which the park is named, the
offshore rocks at Seal Rocks State Recreation Site also host sea lions,
along with numerous species of seabirds, including cormorants,
scoters, harlequins, oystercatchers, turnstones, and surfbirds.

▲ Hoarfrost occurs when water vapor, or fog, freezes.
The resulting ice can coat everything—including trees such
as this graceful one in Jefferson County—touching each twig and
blade of grass with magic to create a virtual fairyland.

▲ Built in the 1930s as a WPA project, Timberline Lodge was
dedicated in 1937 by President Franklin D. Roosevelt. Situated at
six thousand feet on the south slope of Mount Hood in Oregon's
Cascade Range, the lodge is now a National Historic Landmark.
▶▶ Devils Elbow Beach is just one of the attractions at
Heceta Head Lighthouse State Scenic Viewpoint.

▲ Cascade Head provides a stunning view of the Salmon River
estuary. Estuaries are very important ecosystems for marine life. The water
of an estuary, made brackish by a constant flow of tides that mix fresh and salt
waters, furnishes a nutrient-dense environment for a wide variety of sea life.

▶ Filtering through the fog at Seal Rocks State Recreation Site, early
morning light lends a ghostly appearance to the weathered trees.

◄ All along the coast, one of the best times for wave-watching
is after a storm, when towering waves often explode against rocks near
shore. Always in flux, seascapes range from thundering waves to peaceful sunsets.
▲ Huge rocks rise from the sands at Bandon State Natural Area. Bandon offers great
fossil- and rock-hunting opportunities during winter and spring—but beware of
angry seas! The steamer *Acme,* destroyed offshore in 1924, remains buried here.

▲ In late afternoon, the sun's slant highlights intricate
designs on the sand dunes at the Pistol River State Scenic Viewpoint,
near Cape Sebastian. Wind creates ripples in the sand, and wind—along with
the area's unique beach and surf—has made this site the choice for the
National Ocean Windsurfing Championships for several years.

▲ Wild calla *(Calla palustris)* blooms in the Siuslaw National Forest along the Cape Perpetua Trail system. Also known as water arum, swamp robin, or water dragon, wild calla flourishes in the cool, damp environment of the coastal forest floor.

▲ Near Medford, pear trees share space with
mustard plants—both species in glorious bloom.
When planted alongside fruit trees, mustard is thought
to stimulate the trees' growth, but so far, research
has neither proved nor disproved this theory.

▲▲ Portland's Waterfront Park stretches for twenty-
two blocks along the Willamette River. Conceived in the
early 1900s, the park did not become a reality until 1978.
▲ Blueberries flourish in the Iowa Hills area of the Willamette Valley.
Oregon ranks third in the nation in production of blueberries.

▲ In Oregon's lush Willamette Valley,
cool evenings in summer and early fall translate
into deliciously high acid levels in ripening winegrapes.
► Mount Angel Abbey, founded in 1882 by monks from a seven-
hundred-year-old Benedictine monastery in Engelberg,
Switzerland, still thrives in the Willamette Valley.

◀ Starfish, barnacles, and blue mussels cling to rocks near Cannon Beach.
Though they may share the same rock, the three are very different: with no
front or back, starfish can move in any direction without turning; blue mussels
anchor themselves to rocks and pilings with tough, brown fibers that project from one
side of their shells; barnacles, free-swimming as larvae, are permanently fixed as adults.
▲ Surf crashes onto the rocks at Yachats Ocean Road State Natural Site. One of three state
parks in the Yachats area, the natural site encompasses seventy-nine acres.

▲ A family rests by a tractor in a multicolored tulip field at
Iverson's thirty-acre Wooden Shoe Tulip Farm in Woodburn.
Each year for a month, beginning about the first day of spring, the
Wooden Shoe's Tulip Festival charms thousands of visitors
from all over the state and around the country.

▲ Retired logging equipment rests among ferns at the
Merten Sawmill Site in the Opal Creek Scenic Recreation
Area. The steam engine from the battleship USS *Oregon* once
powered logging operations here in the Willamette National Forest.
▶▶ The cliffs at Shore Acres State Park offer excellent vantage
points for viewing the sea in all its varying moods.

◄ The historic Jackson County Courthouse
is now home to the Jacksonville Museum. Erected in
1883, the two-story red brick building served as the courthouse
until 1927 when the county government was moved to Medford.
▲ Situated at Sunny Valley in southwestern Oregon's Josephine
County, the Grave Creek Covered Bridge, constructed
in 1920, incorporates Gothic-style windows.

▲ The Hughes Flying Boat, or "Spruce Goose," flew its
maiden—and only—flight in 1947. More than 218 feet long
with a wingspan of 320 feet, the twentieth century's largest plane
is now displayed at the Evergreen Aviation Museum in McMinnville.
▶ A beautifully decorated saddle typifies the St. Paul Rodeo, first
held July 4, 1936. The year-round population of St. Paul is only
about 400, but the rodeo fills the arena's 10,500 seats.

◄ Towering 14,162 feet above sea level, California's
Mount Shasta is visible from Oregon's Mount Ashland at
the intersection of the Siskiyou Mountains and the Cascades.
▲ With an annual snowfall of approximately two hundred inches, the
Mount Ashland Ski Area provides plenty of opportunity
for good skiing and snowboarding.

▲ Vista House, built as a memorial to Oregon
pioneers, was completed in 1918. The stone building, set
atop a promontory some seven hundred feet above the Columbia
River, is listed in the National Register of Historic Places.
▶ In autumn, bigleaf maple leaves create an artist's palette
along the scenic Historic Columbia River Highway.

◄ With a total drop of 620 feet, Multnomah Falls is the second-
highest year-round waterfall in the nation. Its source is near the summit
of Larch Mountain, four thousand feet above the Columbia River Highway.
▲ A footbridge crosses Multnomah Falls seventy feet above the
splash pool at the base of the upper falls. The lower
falls, shown here, drop sixty-nine feet.

▲ Countless falls, from unnamed seasonal
trickles to year-round cascades, accent the Columbia
River Gorge National Scenic Area. One of the permanent ones,
224-foot Latourell Falls, is accented by snow, icicles, and yellow lichen.
▶ Winter in the Columbia Gorge—always beautiful but sometimes
harsh—is evidenced here by the icicle-encrusted 176-foot
Horsetail Falls in the National Scenic Area.

◄ Each autumn, the spectacular Columbia River
Gorge is a favorite destination for thousands of leaf-watchers.
▲ A small, unnamed stream rushes over boulders on its way to join the mighty Columbia.
►► Mount Hood towers above fruit orchards. A mild climate, abundant
rains most years, and rich soils have made Oregon one of the
nation's largest centers for the production of food.

▲ The Columbia River Gorge is known for its world-class
windsurfing. The river current, flowing from the east, is counter-
balanced during much of spring and summer by strong winds
from the west, creating ideal windsurfing conditions.

▲ Lush flora—here including ferns and dame's rock
(Hesperis matronalis)—is just one of the reasons why, in
1986, the U.S. Congress enacted a law designating the
Columbia River Gorge as a National Scenic Area.

▲ Balsam root *(Balsamorhize deltoidea)* adds
brilliance to a hillside in the foothills of the Cascades.
▶ The waters of Wahkeena Falls twist and turn as they tumble
242 feet over the rocks. Some historians allege that the falls were named
for the daughter of an Indian chief; others say *wahkeena* is a
Yakima Indian word meaning "most beautiful."

◄ Colorful rocks line the East Fork of Hood River,
which provides water to the fruit orchards of Hood River
Valley. The river flows from Mount Hood to the Columbia River.
▲ Near Rowena, in an exposed area of the Columbia River Gorge,
poplar trees *(Populus nigra)* are planted along the edges of
orchards to protect the fragile fruit-bearing trees from the
fierce winds that funnel through the gorge region.

▲▲ Canada geese *(Branta canadensis)* soar in a crisp blue winter
sky. Several subspecies of Canada geese winter in the western states,
including Oregon, returning north each spring to nest and raise their young.
▲ At 11,237 feet, Mount Hood is the tallest mountain in Oregon.
▶ Composed of lava flows, domes, and volcaniclastic deposits,
Mount Hood is popular for a variety of sports, including
skiing, depicted here at Timberline Ski Area.

◄ Set in the Cascades at an elevation of 4,644 feet,
Big Lake is backdropped by 7,794-foot Mount Washington.
▲ Sunset lends the blush of alpenglow to 10,495-foot
Mount Jefferson in the Central Cascades.

▲ In Mount Hood National Forest, vine maple *(Acer circinatum)* glows red in autumn.
▶ The Middle Sister (10,050 feet) and North Sister (10,090 feet) rise above McKenzie
Pass lava flows. Affording views of the flows, today's highway replaces a toll road
constructed by pioneer citizens. Running between the towns of Sisters
and Blue River, the highway reaches an elevation of 5,325 feet.

◄ Snow-covered trees line the banks of the Santiam River. Beginning in the
Central Cascades, the Santiam joins the Willamette River just north of Albany.
▲ The Metolius River plunges over Wizard Falls on its way to join the Deschutes.
►► The Painted Hills are part of John Day Fossil Beds National Monument.
The weathering of volcanic ash has created rock layers of red, pink,
bronze, tan, and black. In spring, bee plant *(Cleome lutea)*
adds bright yellow and green to the mix.

▲ Mount Thielsen, 9,182 feet high, has an unusual pinnacle or spire
that forms its summit. Diamond Lake, at an elevation of 5,182 feet, lies
between Mounts Thielsen and Bailey in the heart of the Umpqua National Forest.
▶ Sparks Lake holds a reflection of the South Sister. At 10,358 feet,
the South Sister is the highest of the Three Sisters.

◄ Seen from across an icy Upper Klamath Lake,
9,495-foot Mount McLoughlin is partly obscured by clouds.
▲ A grove of ponderosa pine *(Pinus ponderosa)* is just one of the attractions
enjoyed by the more than eight million people who visit the Deschutes National Forest
each year. Besides sight-seeing, numerous recreational activities—including
skiing, snowboarding, camping, fishing, hiking, and hunting—also abound.

▲▲ A schoolhouse sits abandoned in
the midst of a field of golden wheat in Wasco County.
▲ The Fall River gets its name from a series of small falls and cascades about
halfway down its eight- to ten-mile length before it meets the Deschutes River.
▶ Workers harvest wheat on the steep hills of Wasco County. Nationwide,
Oregon ranks eighth in the production of wheat.

◄ Designated "fly-fishing only," Hosmere Lake is just
one of many freshwater basins along the Cascade Lakes Highway.
▲ A branch of ponderosa pine *(Pinus ponderosa)* sparkles with morning
dew in Deschutes National Forest. Besides beauty, the national forest
provides a variety of commodities, ranging from timber to
mushroom gathering, from mining to grazing.

▲ Waving gold in the breeze, wheat thrives in the rich soil of
north-central Oregon. Some thirty miles north of the Columbia
River, in Washington, 12,276-foot Mount Adams dominates the horizon.
▶ Seen from the viewpoint at the Ray Atkeson Memorial at Sparks Lake, 9,065-foot Bachelor
Butte towers above Goose Creek, which meanders through a golden meadow.
▶▶ Backdropped by the South and Middle Sisters, aspens shimmer
along the shore of Phalarope Lake at Black Butte Ranch.

◄ Starting from Lava Lake high in the
Cascade Mountains, the Deschutes River flows
for fifty-six miles before cascading down Shears Falls.
▲ A wooden logging wheel waits at the Historic Collier
Memorial State Park, which features an outdoor
museum of historic logging equipment.

▲ Snow highlights animal tracks near
Fort Rock State Natural Area. Fort Rock, whose
walls rise 325 feet above the surrounding countryside,
is an old shield volcano set in what was once a shallow sea.
▶ Smith Rock State Park's dramatic cliffs and spires rise
above the Crooked River. Rock climbers from all over
the nation enjoy challenging the sheer walls.

◄ Aspens splash bright color on the slopes of Steens Mountain.
▲ Near Baker City, cattle graze peacefully beneath the Elkhorn Mountains.
►► A working ranch nestles in the shadow of the Wallowa Mountains. Sometimes
referred to as "America's Little Switzerland," the Wallowas contrast white
granite peaks with brilliant alpine meadows, and luxuriant green forests
give relief along the banks of shimmering lakes and streams.

▲ The Deschutes River affords numerous opportunities for
boating, fishing, rafting, and camping along its hundred-mile length.

▶ Flora, ranging from sagebrush *(Artemisia tridentata)* to a variety of
wildflowers, dots the high desert near the town of Plush in southeastern Oregon.

▶▶ Sunrise lends a pastel wash to the parched floor of the Alvord Desert. Located in the
southeast corner of the state, the Alvord encompasses approximately twenty-five
thousand acres and receives rainfall of only about eight to ten inches annually.